Destroy the Cage

By Jamillah Cupe

Other Books By Jamillah Cupe
- ❖ Un-Stuckness Breaking Generational Chains and Strongholds Through Prayer

- ❖ Un-Stuckness Keys To Deliverance Through Prayer Jesus' Way

Journal Article
Hardships Children Face in the United States of America by Having a Parent In Prison: How To Help Them! A Program Proposal. *Social Criminology*, 137(4). doi:10.4172/2375-4435.1000137

Workshop Topics
- ❖ Healing
- ❖ Dealing with a crisis
- ❖ Addressing root offenses
- ❖ Breaking cycles of abuse
- ❖ The power in prayer
- ❖ Prayer strategies
- ❖ Strategies to break bloodline strongholds
- ❖ Ways to manifest deliverance
- ❖ Restructuring the foundation of your family
- ❖ Child development
- ❖ Parenting techniques
- ❖ Communication techniques
- ❖ How to pray effectively
- ❖ Goal Setting

To Schedule Speaking Engagement
Send invitation request to: info@jamillahcupe.com

Dedication

I dedicate this book to my children Da'Borah, Mirandah, Anaiah and Josiah.

Table of Contents

Special Thanks

Thank you to all those who have been spiritually supportive, especially my Godmother Regina Russell.

To my grandmother Eleanor Cupe and father Booker Clark for raising me.

To my Great Uncle, Pastor Willie Cupe for encouraging me to surrender all and live a life pleasing to God. Also, for teaching me to eat spiritually as often as I eat physically and to run to God first instead of man. I honor and love you Man of God!

To Aunt Zora Hicks who taught me true power comes from reading and studying the word of God; I miss you.

To great grandmother Ruth Moody, for inspiring my walk in the ministry.

To my Spiritual Father Pastor Benny F. Smith for your spiritual guidance.

To Avada Oatman Smith A.KA. Nana Doll for being a spiritual grandmother, always keeping me encouraged in the ministry.

Dr. Denise William Johnson who planted seeds of faith into my life. When I was facing death, you spoke life.

This Book Is Anointed To Deliver and Set Free! I Pray You the Reader, Will Hear the Holy Spirit Voice Louder Than Mine or Any Other. May God Bless You and Keep You Totally Wrapped in His Peace and Protection, In All Times of Life; For There Is a Time For Everything. I Decree This Is Your Time To move Forward Into God's Purpose. Who the Son Set Free is Free Indeed! I Thank God For Jesus!

Dear Father God,

Your Words Are Like Fire.

For You Are A Consuming Fire,

Let Your Fire Be Upon Me,

Burning Everything Away,

That Does Not Give You Glory, Purify

My Flesh Into Ashes.

May Your Words

Forever Blaze In My Heart,

Until I am An

Ignited Flame and Fire,

You Created Me To Be.

By Jamillah Cupe

Introduction

Importance of Prayer

This book is being written as an encouragement for children of God to embrace a life of intense prayer and elevate in faith, especially during trying times. Further, it is to inspire new Christian Believers to not become weary in following the teachings of Jesus Christ.

I've encountered many individuals who have become discouraged, because they felt as if their prayers were unheard or not answered. There are many benefits in being a Child of God and serving God in spirit and truth but those who do not have knowledge of their authority, may think otherwise.

To get the best from this book, it should be read

entirely because I do not rush the information. I go from topic to the next, in hope that you will gain understanding from the overall solid message.

Prayer is essential in our daily living as a way to honor God, give Him thanks and address all matters that center around our life. The application of prayer, also leads us into closeness with God, strengthens us spiritually and is a buffer against emotional breakdowns.

The act and power of prayer protects us from harm, breaks curses, destroys demonic oppressions, moves mountains, makes peace appear in the mist of storms, brings healing to our mind, spirit and soul, as well as our bodies, according to our faith.

Prayer especially with use of the scriptures is medicine, like no other you would ever find! Proverbs 3:8 tells us that the word of God is health to our bodies and nourishment to our bones. In Prayer we become restored, break strongholds and enforce God's will in our lives.

There is exceedingly great power that comes with having your life centered by a persistent prayer régime and meditation on the word of God. There will be no breakthroughs or deliverance without it. Your achievements in life are outcomes of what you say, speak, believe and put action into; things spoken with focus is prayer, even silently in the heart.

The Chapter of Job 14 tells us that man born of a woman is of few days and born of trouble and in the book of John Jesus teaches that we all are going to have trials and tribulations but to not be discouraged for he has made a way that leads to peace and victory. Many afflictions suffer the righteous but the Lord is faithful and delivers us from them all. Taking us from testimony to testimony and teaching us to grow from faith to faith.

With all the hardships and challenges that come in the experience of life itself, you cannot address spiritual problems with physical approaches, in an effort to cope, cover up, avoid or block reality; things such as anger, hate, shame, anxiety, depression, fear, resentment, joy, happiness, excitement, and love are all spiritually felt and expressed out emotionally.

You cannot see or touch these things physically, but can feel them 100% strongly in your spirit. No one can tell you that whatever emotions you are experiencing aren't true, or do not exist because they don't see it inside of you! Who can look at you and see 90 lbs. of depressions, 50 lbs. of fear or 100 lbs. of hurt?

A lot of times one can walk with their head held up and other people looking at them would not have a clue as to what is really going on inside of that person, due to assumptions or prejudgments of the outer appearance. With God you cannot see him either, but I promise you, if you seek Him you will find Him and feel His presence; and in this experience, no one will be able to tell you otherwise either!

If negative emotions (such as fear, anxiety, depression, anger) are harbored for too long, they can lead to emotional imbalances (confusion, mental stress), spiritual imbalances and physical sickness (sleep problems, high blood pressure, heart problems, diabetes, stomach issues, hair loss) and much more. Regrettably not addressed quickly, these entertained energies can create everything out of order in your life on multiple levels and God is a God of order.

People who use physical approaches to address spiritual trauma, pain and disappointments by use of displaying pity, having a victim mentality, drug abuse, alcohol abuse, mistreating others, manipulating and practicing any form of addictions, will remain stuck in Satan's cycle. Quick fixes as such cannot produce any real lifetime permanent solutions.

One has to really be tired of being tired of dealing with stagnation forces and have a made-up mind that they want to seek, happiness and be willing to spiritually push for it; by praying sincerely with all their might and seeking God for it. A man's life becomes outwardly what they internally feel and/or believe (Prov.23:7).

For this reason, it is important to be balanced mentally and keep your mind connected to God as you go through every experience in life. God should be kept first in all that you do. The lord must order your every step. For you to hear His directions concerning your life you must be mentally and spiritually in tune. Sheep's must hear and know the voice of their Shepherd.

Throughout the Bible, those who sought God, received directions from him and lived a life that included submitting and prayer. Even Jesus Christ our savior used prayer as a tool in His own life and he was the living word made flesh.

As children of God we must develop a life of constant prayer that comes naturally and have tough/consistent faith. Some people pray and feel like their prayers are unheard by God. Some people pray and worry. Some people pray and don't believe.

I was once all of the above. It was not until I became extremely tired of facing constant cycles of being in a storm and at my wit's end emotionally, that I totally surrendered and decided that I will stop crying, stop complaining, but instead go through the fire if I had too, knowing that God will still be with me even if my fight was in hell. I was determined that if fighting was my only option, I would fight well and make the enemy backup off of me!

It was during this time I began to pray like my life depended on it, because I knew it did. I would pray until I was tired and then reflect on how much I had been through and then start praying all over again. When it looked like I was tired, I would demand my total deliverance in every area of my life and family and find the strength to pray some more.

This was the start of me praying 4 hours plus every day, without even realizing how long I was praying. I even let go trying to keep my children's father and chose to let him go. God became the primary relationship I wanted more than anything. I knew that man could not keep me, love me and help me like God. Man, often has conditions for how they love, accept and treat you anyway.

I just wanted God to change my life and grant me a breakthrough; I refused to let anything stand in my way. I was running to God with all my mind, thoughts, prayers, worship, fasting, studying and meditating— I wanted to live and not die! Plus, my children needed me to live also. Hypothesizing that there had to be more out of life than just pain. I placed no time limit when praying but prayed until I felt God move.

As my prayer life increased, I tell you things began to change in my spirit and life; I was seeing it and feeling it. Getting off work at midnight, often I prayed between 12:40am – 3:30am, after my son was picked up for school 7:40am-11am and throughout the day while doing chores. The Holy Spirit began to teach me the order of praying, what to pray and how to pray.

My prayer themes often fell into two areas (1) worshiping my way into prayer and (2) warfare prayers that uproot, place boundaries and restrictions (on negative forces that wanted to keep me in a cycle so that I did not prosper). I also learned how to truly worship and fall in love with the presence of God.

It seems when you are born with a great purpose the

enemy tries to bring so many situations your way so that you will become more distracted by your problem situations than praying and worshiping God. The key is to not be moved by distractions, feelings and emotions but shifting your focus on the one who is able to solve all problems.

Even that one issue that you think is impossible for God to fix; it's not. He is more than able to do it! In life we are always going to have trials and tribulations (John 16:33). However, keeping your faith and trust in God no matter what, will allow you to have constant victories; I mean bold and unshakable faith in God!

There are certain things that can hinder prayers from being answered: doubt, blame, disbelief, lack of faith, fear, failure to take responsibility, disobedience, un-forgiveness, and negative emotions/feelings are a few of them; God does not operate in these forces the enemy does.

The aforementioned are all characteristics of spiritual weights that keep you bound. They have to be addressed if your hope is to elevate in prayer, and see how praying in faith can change many things, in ALL areas of your life. Spiritual/emotional weights will hold you down and keep you physically, emotionally and spiritually stuck; these things must be released and let go, through prayer with the application of faith.

Prayer and use of faith is at the center of everything we do as children of God. It's how we talk to and hear from God, it is sacred and it builds our faith, to grow strong as the tree that is grown from that little mustard seed. We use it when putting on the whole armor of God; it is the foundational ingredient in all declarations and decrees.

It is utilized when binding, loosing, giving commands and the list can go on and on. Prayer is a powerful tool and should be done with expectation and demonstration that you have faith and trust in God, no matter what things look like. You cannot effectively operate in the kingdom of God without it.

Question, can you imagine being in a relationship with someone you depend on, but don't trust? That relationship will be weak because of its foundation. A weak foundation cannot stand against storms and sooner or later it will break; it must be built correctly and strong. Value, trust and commitment is necessary.

The same is true with prayer and in trusting God. You have to have a strong secure foundation in the Lord or else the enemy will enter into any crack and eat at the base, to steal, kill and destroy your peace of mind and confidence in God by creating fear, doubt and mistrust.

If you are a Christian believer who, after accepting Jesus Christ as your Lord and Savior, automatically began to experience an increase of problems, this prayer book is for you! If you believe your prayers are not being answered, then this book is most definitely for you!

This book will firstly review foundational knowledge showing who you are as a child of God. In hope to encourage your focus on God and in faith while praying; so that the breakthrough you desire will be received.

As long as your mind is renewed daily: on who God is, His promises, who you are as His child, the power in pleading the Blood of Jesus, the importance of being saturated in the word of God no matter the trial or tribulation, you will walk through the fire and not be burned, nor will its smoke consume you. The cage in your mind will be broken.

Your cage can be fear, unbelief, doubt, ignorance, hopelessness, and/or anything that places limits or barriers on your abundant life through Christ Jesus and the mighty power of God. There is nothing that can restrict the power and movement of God in your life, **except** your unbelief.

The power of God and move of His awesomeness cannot be caged, especially not in man's box they often give Him. I am sure you have heard God don't/would not do that, God won't work like that, deliverance don't work that way, he won't accept Jesus, he's Muslim and etc. Failure to understand that God moves mysteriously in His OWN way and choosing, will keep you in a cage.

We cannot control how God moves, heals, set free, delivers and operate in a box. He is the God of all possibilities. It's the power of God that does the healing, saving, deliverance and set the captives free. Even though one maybe walking on a wrong path, it is not their final path or destination. Only God knows their beginning, between and end of their journey.

The magnitude of our Lord is bigger and greater than any problem or challenge, far beyond man's comprehension. God created everything that exist before you seen and unseen, you breathe from His breath, do you really think He cannot help you or revealing Himself to someone of a different religion or lifestyle would be a challenge for Him?

An enemy's advantage is knowing the weakness and ignorance of his opponent and Satan wants us to stay in the dark of how our God truly moves. Also, oblivious to how he moves and to our God given power over him.

God wants His children to be awake instead of sleep, aware rather than distracted and blind, knowledgeable as opposed to clueless. You have to really know what Jesus Christ did for you when he died on the cross and rose on the 3rd day. What He did gives us all the opportunity to receive salvation and to no longer be a slave to sin.

Let me ask, do you recognize your new birth and what it means? Do you understand that your first birth was that of the flesh; however, your new birth is that of the Spirit, through Christ Jesus (2 Corinthians 5:17). Therefore, if any man be in Christ, he is a new creature: old things are passed away; behold, all things are become new (John 1:13; 1John 3:9). God's children are made new.

God wants His children to wake up and take their rightful positions and authority in knowing who they are. He wants us to use the tools and instructions he provided at hand. Hosea 4:6 informs us that people perish because of ignorance and as children of God, not knowing who you are, can cause you to perish spiritually, as well. Not having a vision also leads to the same end (Proverbs 29:18). For it is only in knowing the truth that we are truly free (John 8:23).

Chapter One
Do You Know Who You Are?

Let me ask, do you know who you are as a child of God? (John 1:12 But as many as received Him, to them He gave the right to become children of God, even to those who believe in His name, who were born, not of blood nor of the will of the flesh nor of the will of man, but of God). If you do not know who you are, you will always have identity insecurities.

As children of God, we are reborn into the family of Jesus Christ, made new in Him, abiding in Him and He in us. Do you believe great is our God that lives on the inside of us then he that is in the world (2 Corinthians, Romans 12:5, John 15:5, 1 Corinthians 6:19, 1John 4:4)? Knowing and believing this is very important. How can you be afraid when God is with you?

Do you know what you are entitled to as a Son or Daughter of God? (Romans 8:17 And if children, then heirs; heirs of God, and joint-heirs with Christ; if so be that we suffer with him, that we may be also glorified together). You cannot enforce or operate in what you do not know you have.

You are entitled to receive your inheritance, which is everything Jesus Christ sacrificed His life for you to receive: salvation, restoration, redemption, healing, power and prosperity in every area of your life. To be one with Jesus as He is one with the father (John 17:21-23).

It is good to know that as a child of God, greater is the God that lives on the inside of us than any challenge we may face in the world. God and His word that resides in us fights for us. We are more than conquerors through Christ Jesus, we have victory and liberation through Him! The scriptures below show that when Jesus died on the cross, He redeemed us:

Galatians 3:13-14 *[13] Christ hath redeemed us from the curse of the law, being made a curse for us: for it is written, cursed is every one that hangeth on a tree: [14] That the blessing of Abraham might come on the Gentiles through Jesus Christ; that we might receive the promise of the Spirit through faith.* Whoever receives Jesus and believes in the power of His name He gave them power to become sons of God (John 1:12). In your new birth you have been accepted into the family of Jesus Christ. All old things have passed away behold all things are now new for those who are in Christ Jesus and The Spirit of God dwells inside of you. Our flesh (body, first birth of water) must die with Christ and our new birth (second birth of the spirit) must rise with Christ (John 3:1-21).

Romans 8:2 *[2] For the law of the Spirit of life in Christ Jesus hath made me free from the law of sin and death.*

John 1:12 *[12] But as many as received him, to them gave he power to become the sons of God, even to them that believe on his name:*

Colossians 1:13-14 *[13]Who hath delivered us from the power of darkness, and hath translated us into the kingdom of his dear Son: [14]In whom we have redemption through his blood, even the forgiveness of sins:*

Romans 8:8-14 *[8] So then they that are in the flesh cannot please God.[9] But ye are not in the flesh, but in the Spirit, if so be that the Spirit of God dwell in you. Now if any man have not the Spirit of Christ, he is none of His.[10] And if Christ be in you, the body is dead because of sin; but the Spirit is life because of righteousness.[11] But if the Spirit of him that raised up Jesus from the dead dwell in you, he that raised up Christ from the dead shall also quicken your mortal bodies by His Spirit that dwelleth in you. [12]Therefore, brethren, we are debtors, not to the flesh, to live after the flesh. [13]For if ye live after the flesh, ye shall die: but if ye through the Spirit do mortify the deeds of the body, ye shall live. [14]For as many as are led by the Spirit of God, they are the sons of God.*

1 John 5:1 *[1]Whosoever believeth that Jesus is the Christ is born of God: and every one that loveth him that begat loveth him also that is begotten of him.*

John 14:1-31 *Let not your heart be troubled: ye believe in God, believe also in me.[2] In my Father's house are many mansions: if it were not so, I would have told you. I go to prepare a place for you.[3] And if I go and prepare a place for you, I will come again, and receive you unto myself; that where I am, there ye may be also.[4] And whither I go ye know, and the way ye know.[5] Thomas saith unto him, Lord, we know not whither thou goest; and how can we know the way?[6] Jesus saith unto him, I am the way, the truth, and the life: no man cometh unto the Father, but by me.[7] If ye had known me, ye should have known my Father also: and from henceforth ye know him, and have seen him.[8] Philip saith unto him, Lord, show us the Father, and it sufficeth us.[9] Jesus saith unto him, Have I been so long time with you, and yet hast thou not known me, Philip? He that hath seen me hath seen the Father; and how sayest thou then, Show us the Father?[10] Believest thou not that I am in the Father, and the Father in me? the words that I speak unto you I speak not of myself: but the Father that dwelleth in me, he doeth the works.[11] Believe me that I am in the Father, and the Father in me: or else believe me for the very works' sake.[12] Verily, verily, I say unto you, He that believeth on me, the works that I do shall he do also; and greater works than these shall he do; because I go unto my Father.[13] And whatsoever ye shall ask in my name, that will I do, that the*

Father may be glorified in the Son.[14] If ye shall ask any thing in my name, I will do it.[15] If ye love me, keep my commandments.[16] And I will pray the Father, and he shall give you another Comforter, that he may abide with you forever;[17] Even the Spirit of truth; whom the world cannot receive, because it seeth him not, neither knoweth him: but ye know him; for he dwelleth with you, and shall be in you.[18] I will not leave you comfortless: I will come to you.[19] Yet a little while, and the world seeth me no more; but ye see me: because I live, ye shall live also.[20] At that day ye shall know that I am in my Father, and ye in me, and I in you.[21] He that hath my commandments, and keepeth them, he it is that loveth me: and he that loveth me shall be loved of my Father, and I will love him, and will manifest myself to him.[22] Judas saith unto him, not Iscariot, Lord, how is it that thou wilt manifest thyself unto us, and not unto the world?[23] Jesus answered and said unto him, If a man love me, he will keep my words: and my Father will love him, and we will come unto him, and make our abode with him.[24] He that loveth me not keepeth not my sayings: and the word which ye hear is not mine, but the Father's which sent me.[25] These things have I spoken unto you, being yet present with you.[26] But the Comforter, which is the Holy Ghost, whom the Father will send in my name, he shall teach you all things, and bring all things to your remembrance, whatsoever I have said unto you.[27] Peace I leave with you, my peace I give unto you: not as the world giveth, give I unto you. Let not your heart be troubled, neither let it be afraid.[28] Ye have heard how I said unto you, I go away, and come again unto you. If ye loved me, ye would rejoice, because I said, I go unto the Father: for my Father is greater than I.[29] And now I have told you before it come to pass, that, when it is come to pass, ye might believe.[30] Hereafter I will not talk much with you: for the prince of this world cometh, and hath nothing in me .[31] But that the world may know that I love the Father; and as the Father gave me commandment, even so I do. Arise, let us go hence.

These scriptures tell who you are as a child of God and how much God loves us, that He sent Jesus Christ. He loves us so much, that He's not a God that just lives in the sky, He lives on the inside of us (John 14). How awesome if we can just let God be God in our life and trust him in everything.

Even on the things we are not too sure of, we should trust and follow the word of God with confidence. Jesus said He is the way, truth and the life, so even when we don't know the way, in every situation, in trusting Him, the way will be made, as we walk in faith.

Sometimes our problem is that we have to know everything in lieu of having the courage to just walk by faith. If you don't know who you are as a child of God and how you are expected to operate as such, you cannot execute authority, dominion or the power to enforce decrees or operate in faith, as God desires.

You will walk in insecurity, fear, doubt and this will make you into a double minded and unstable person in all your endeavors (James 1:8). Doubt gives room to fear and God has not given us the spirit of fear but of love, power and of a sound mind; you must believe and trust God in everything. You have to trust Him more than man.

Man will fail you even if they have good intentions and really don't mean to not follow through. Anything could get in their way preventing them from keeping their word. God tells his children that it is not wise to completely trust in the arms of man (Jeremiah 17:5; Proverbs 118:8). Man can fail you but failure is not nowhere in God's resume. He never fails!

He allows those who trust and believe in Him to be victorious and grow in levels from trust to trust, faith to faith, glory to glory and strength to strength; to where they cultivate with complete confidence and become strong in Him.

If you do not know the truth, (teachings and promises of Jesus), facts (the word and promises of God) and identity of your rebirth in Jesus Christ, you become at risk for believing a lie, not knowing what to expect, ask for or question, and even worse, vulnerable to the enemy attacks.

SELF REFLECTIONS YOU MAY WANT TO JOURNAL

How do you see yourself? What are your beliefs about yourself (including ways, triggers and personality)? How would someone you live with or is close to you describe you? How would an associate, such as a coworker describe you? What do the Scriptures say about who you are and how God sees you? Do you see yourself as God sees you?

_____
_____
_____
_____
_____
_____
_____
_____
_____
_____
_____
_____
_____
_____
_____
_____
_____
_____
_____
_____
_____
_____
_____

Chapter Two

Do You Know Your Authority?

Do you know your authority, rights, inheritance, power and tools available to assist you? If you do not know who you are in Christ Jesus and the things you are entitled to, you will not make it spiritually. You have to know your royal heritage and how to operate in it. What you don't know you cannot request or enforce.

Also, what you don't know would definitely keep you caged, preventing you from growth, elevation, opportunities and blessings. God wants His children to be wise, knowledgeable and understand how to effectively operate in His kingdom. Without knowledge there's no way you can live prosperous and strategically counteract against demonic plans of the enemy.

It is not God's desire that you remain in a position where the enemy can steal, kill and destroy your inheritance, prosperity, healing, deliverance and breakthroughs, all because you don't know your rightful authority and how to operate in it. Lack of knowledge keeps you in darkness and will cause your life to perish quickly (Hosea 4:6).

God did not send Jesus Christ for you to remain a victim, you must become a Victor! When you began to walk and operate in who you are with your rightful authority, you will see life, your past and present, trials and tribulations much differently. It is essential to be confident in knowing and trust God.

Luke 10:18-19 *[18] And he said unto them, I beheld Satan as lightning fall from heaven. [19] Behold, I give unto you power to tread on serpents and scorpions, and over all the power of the enemy: and nothing shall by any means hurt you.*

Colossians 1:13 *[13] Who hath delivered us from the power of darkness, and hath translated us into the kingdom of his dear Son:*

John 15:7 *7 If ye abide in me, and my words abide in you, ye shall ask what ye will, and it shall be done unto you.*

Mark 16 15-18 *15 And he said unto them, Go ye into all the world, and preach the gospel to every creature. 16 He that believeth and is baptized shall be saved; but he that believeth not shall be damned. 17 And these signs shall follow them that believe; In my name shall they cast out devils; they shall speak with new tongues; 18 They shall take up serpents; and if they drink any deadly thing, it shall not hurt them; they shall lay hands on the sick, and they shall recover).*

Ephesians 6:10-18 *10 Finally, my brethren, be strong in the Lord, and in the power of his might. 11 Put on the whole armour of God, that ye may be able to stand against the wiles of the devil. 12 For we wrestle not against flesh and blood, but against principalities, against powers, against the rulers of the darkness of this world, against spiritual wickedness in high places 13 Wherefore take unto you the whole armour of God, that ye may be able to withstand in the evil day, and having done all, to stand. 14 Stand therefore, having your loins girt about with truth, and having on the breastplate of righteousness; 15 And your feet shod with the preparation of the gospel of peace; 16 Above all, taking the shield of faith, wherewith ye shall be able to quench all the fiery darts of the wicked. 17 And take the helmet of salvation, and the sword*

47

of the Spirit, which is the word of God: [18] Praying always with all prayer and supplication in the Spirit, and watching thereunto with all perseverance and supplication for all saints.

As children of God we should aim to have the mind of Christ. For this reason, the scripture says "let this mind be in thee that is also in Christ Jesus and as Jesus taught, ye shall know the truth and the truth shall set you free (John 8:23)."

Your life cannot become liberated without knowing the truth. In addition, not walking in the mind of knowing the truth of who you are and your given authority as a child of God, can lead you to become spiritually vulnerable. Furthermore, it makes it easier for Satan to have a greater advantage in stealing, killing and destroying your peace, joy, health, family, relationships and everything related to your self-image, goals, vision and more.

Satan wants you to stay in the dark, in hope that you never come into the light of knowing who you truly are or learn how to exercise your authority to over him. He does not want you to recognize your power and wants you to think you're powerless and he is in control—this is a lie, far from the truth! You already have the victory and Satan place is under your feet; make him stay there.

For the Bible says that people perish because of a lack of knowledge (Hosea 4:6). We cannot be wise of the enemy devices nor enforce the promises and will of God in ignorance. Nor become strong in the Lord and in the power of His might with a weak bible study (word knowledge), faith, prayer life and not knowing your rightful position and authority in the Kingdom of God.

This is why reading, deeply studying, praying, believing in faith and meditating on the word of God, are foundational principles that should be done daily and as often as possible. You must build up on the word and ensure that it resides on the inside of you. Practicing these things daily will strengthen and help you to receive an impartation of God's wisdom and knowledge deeply.

In addition, reveal your awareness of what you can do in and through Christ Jesus. Anyone who wears an armor or combat uniform, must practice how to operate with wearing the gear and effectively utilize the fighting strategies, tools and weapons, to where it becomes second nature. In this type of situation, knowing or not knowing how to properly operate the armor and weapons, can mean the difference between staying alive or dying.

The same is true in putting on the armor of God. Whether or not you have confidence in knowing everything that pertains to wearing the armor and rules of warfare, could determine if you will remain alive or die spiritually. When armor is place on one must be ready to fight and win. Knowledge, experience, confidence and skills allows a solider to elevate to a higher rank, power and authority. Moving them from one level into the next.

You must let the seeds of knowledge, wisdom, understanding, diligent practice and studying, along with faith not fall on stony ground. If your roots in God do not run deep you will not be able to stand strong in God's armor. When the fight of trials and tribulations come, you will be spiritually destroyed. Your roots must be strong and connected deep in the foundation of God.

For this reason, obtaining knowledge and wisdom, by study, prayer and meditation further inspires our faith, truth and trust in God to increase. This helps us as his children to grow from faith to faith, strength to strength and glory to glory. Knowledge and wisdom go hand and hand. You must know your instructions from the Lord.

Having knowledge is invaluable but not knowing how to apply it in your daily life, makes it worthless. The word of God and the Holy Spirit provides knowledge and wisdom (James 1:5; Proverbs 2:6). In like manner, prayer is one of the many tools of spiritual weaponry that God has given you for use to apply spiritual enforcement (Ephesians 6).

The use of knowledge and wisdom concurrently aids one to become prosperous not only in prayer but in every area of life: it fosters individual growth (physically, mentally, spiritually, financially) with the ability to disrupt all forms of disunity and anti-love tactics of the enemy. We can pray things in and/or out of our lives.

Not knowing who you are and your authority, can leave you spiritually weak in your faith. If you don't know the facts of any whole situation, you could believe any lie being told or shown, and walk in fear for no reason, other than not knowing the truth. The enemy will love if you do this! For he loves manipulating and creating illusions that influence confusion.

Satan's advantage is our lack of wisdom and knowledge. Children of God must have a strong spiritual approach to reject the schemes Satan tries to use in order to keep us in bondage. Jesus prayed that those who accepted him will be sanctified by TRUTH and further identifies that the Word of God is Truth, (John 17:17).

In addition, Psalms 119:9 says we are made clean by the Word of God. Truth is, we need knowledge, wisdom and understanding of who we are in God's Kingdom as His Children and joint heirs with Christ (Romans 8:17).

Prayer can be seen as a combination of words with meaning, expression, statements and thoughts, with intent and desires; but when combined with scriptures and an intent or purpose, becomes even stronger prayers. The Holy Bible shows that the Word is foundational in how God operates. In the beginning was the Word and the Word was God and the Word was with God, remember (John 1).

The Word was always in the beginning with God and without it nothing was made that existed (read Genesis, Isaiah & John). We have to study, eat and breathe the Word to know the Word, use the Word and apply the Word in our prayers, commands, decrees and declarations, as well as when exercising authority. God has given us authority to speak words of life or death (Proverbs 18:21).

I have learned that as an unwanted situation and/or report occurs, immediately with likewise speed, rebuke and speak words of life to it. The enemy, the father of lies and illusions will often create situations to deter and distract you from staying focused in the vision of who you are in your power and authority.

It is not only from a lack of knowledge can we perish but from a lack of vision, as well (Proverbs 29:18). Satan can make something look true when it actually isn't. He operates on creating lies and illusions that the physical eyes can see. For this reason, we must not let our guard down and intentionally walk by faith and not by sight.

It's critical to train yourself to immediately present and give every situation to God, instantly! Further, enforce it by speaking the word of God to the bad report or situation. We must not be moved, afraid, shaken or intimidated by (what things appear to be/look like, otherwise Satan will have you believe a lie) how people try to mistreat you: the rebellious child, rejection from people/family, offense, the health report and financial matter or any attacks and etc.

As you speak to these mountains, they have to shift from being a problem to a testimony. You can only get to this point by walking in the substance of things hoped for and the evidence of things not seen physically— **FAITH**.

God wants His children to operate in strong faith, using His words in praying, making declarations and decrees over our life, for it is the sword of the spirit and our tool to cut down and destroy spiritual barriers, limitations and wickedness. God has given us authority to use his words in prayer, declarations, decrees, giving commands, placing restrictions, operating in faith, speaking life to a situation that looks dead or impossible and placing angels on assignment.

We cannot operate as children of God in fear, only in faith. We must not be afraid or frightened. Why should we be afraid when we serve a mighty and all-powerful God? When we speak and use the word, we must believe what we say. The words that come out of our mouth are powerful and prayer is powerful! That is why we cannot pray and then speak negative and add doubt to the subject we just prayed for and spoke life to.

We must use our words to speak prosperity into our life and to dismiss hindrances, setbacks and interruptions and/or not be moved by situations. We don't have to accept everything that comes in our life as permanent. Our language as children of God is so important and how we use our words is crucial.

Again, it can be a matter of life or death. We should have the language and mind of Jesus Christ, walking in the knowledge of who we are and believing in faith. It is so necessary to have a level of faith in applying knowledge, wisdom and understanding. Nothing can be done well without it.

Faith is an essential tool you need in order to utilize any spiritual weapon God has given for defense; Ephesian 6 states that above all, in placing on the protective armor, applying and using the weapons of God, the key tool is faith. Nothing will work as God intended for you without faith. The ability to place on the armor of God properly is faith and nothing can be used effectively without it.

Only with faith can you fight well and come out of various tribulations victoriously. When the darts of the enemy come towards you, your children or family, your faith will be a shield and shut his schemes and tactics down! Unfortunately, without faith you will fail.

It is the main component in everything you do as a child of God. Faith is like a seed, starting out it can be very small but in time as you continue to trust God, it will grow and grow. All you need in order to operate in faith is to just believe, even if it's just a little. You have to know how to stand on the word of God, and stay persistent in prayer regardless of what you hear or what the report appears to be.

It is your sword of defense and allows God's word to be alive and active working in, through and around you, and working exceedingly well with faith (Hebrews 4:12- *12 For the word of God is quick, and powerful, and sharper than any two-edged sword, piercing even to the dividing asunder of soul and spirit, and of the joints and marrow, and is a discerner of the thoughts and intents of the heart).*

Prayer is one of the methods with which you have to rigorously stand your ground, to enforce the word of God and His promises in your life. This prevents Satan from being able to successfully steal, kill, and destroy your purpose, peace, joy, future and victory.

Satan will always try you, but you cannot let him manipulate your faith or sight. Your eyes must stay fixed on Jesus. When Peter was walking on water, as soon as he took his eyes off of Jesus, he became fearful and began to sink. In every situation, in prayer, it is important to keep your eyes and faith totally fixed on Jesus and not shift your sight to anything else, regardless of what hits or comes against you; don't lose sight of your help.

It could mean the difference between walking and sinking. Let your faith grow in the Lord that you may stand strong in Him. As you remain faithful in small things, in time, with patience your faith will grow. It pleases God when we operate and live strongly by faith. Without knowing and having the wisdom and understanding of who you are as a child of God and the way you should operate as such, you will constantly run to man instead of God and have a life Satan can easily manipulate.

The arms of man can fail you and being in the web of Satan can kill and destroy you. There is a great difference between walking in fear and walking by faith. Satan wants every decision you make in life to be influenced by fear. While on the other hand, God wants you to operate and make choices by faith. Satan operates by attacking the physical sight of children of God, hoping they would move from a position of having faith to being afraid and doubtful.

He makes something appear to be the truth when it's not, is the master of lies and false images, the creator of confusion and chaos, generator of disunity in relationships and families, and supplier of gossip and false representation. In knowing how he operates, you must not be moved from your position by what the eyes see or ears hear, that is not of a good report.

Immediately nip confusion, doubt and fear from

spreading, by operating as a child of God that speaks the Word with authority. Know that you are not waiting for victory to happen, you already have it! What you know you can claim. When you lack revelation of this truth, unfortunately you will feel defeated and believe the enemy lies over the word of God.

What did Jesus Christ do for you? What are your rights?
What is your authority? What are the things you can do to
better operate in your authority as a child of God? What
can you do to grow your faith from a seed to a tree?
What things can you do to shift your weakness into
becoming your strength?

_____
_____
_____
_____
_____
_____
_____
_____
_____
_____
_____
_____
_____
_____
_____
_____
_____
_____
_____
_____
_____
_____
_____
_____

Chapter Three
Two Key Tools In Prayer

There are two certain key tools that are foundational in determining your success in prayer. Moreover, not only in prayer but in warfare, deliverance and in victory in every area of your life. If you learn to embrace them in your daily walk, you would victoriously go very far in life. Nothing would be able to stop you from moving forward into God's purpose.

The two principle things needed are **Faith** and **The Word**. Faith is power and the Word is power. These are the two powers that God used in the beginning to create everything. The Bible tells us that by Faith the worlds were framed by the word of God (2 Peter 3:5; Hebrews 1:3; Heb.11:3). When God spoke commanding words such as "let there be…." What He spoke it became (Gen 1:3-26). The Word was always in the beginning with God and the Word was God, there was nothing made that was made without the Word. All things were made by the Word. The Word is Life and Light. Jesus was the word made flesh and the light of the world (John 1 1-14).

The application of **Faith** and **the Word** are the same two core elements needed when we submit our prayers to God and operate as a Child of God. Remember, God made us in His image and likeness so we cannot fully function in His image and likeness without allowing faith and the word to become a natural part of our being in our daily lives.

Do you know that if we abide in Christ Jesus and His words in us, we can ask anything and it shall be done unto us? Because God's Word cannot return unto him void nor can it return on the inside of His children void (John 15:7; Isaiah 55:11; Colossians 3:16), it has to accomplish what Gods pleases.

As children of God we are supposed to always walk

by faith (2 Cor.5:7) and when we pray our faith should reunite with God's faith and his word. It is faith that pleases God and faith that moves God (Heb. 11:6). God made us in His image and likeness and faith and the word is core of who He is. For this reason, operating in faith and in the word, are foundational principles that must dwell within us as His children.

We should pray in faith and pray in the Word— walk in faith and walk in the word, at all times. In addition, grow in faith and grow in the word; as mature sons and daughters of God. Your choice of words during prayer is a serious matter. You have to be clear on what you're declaring, the boundaries, limitations and blessing/promises you are evoking.

Words during prayer must be strongly intentional and not passive. If you do not fight oppressing situations and forces with the word of God, you will not live life as winner despite already having the victory through Jesus Christ. Victory do not belong to the enemy, so do let him steal it.

FAITH

- **Faith** is defined as the substance of things hoped for; the evidence of things not seen

(Heb.11:1).

- By Grace we are saved through **faith** (Ephesian 2:8).

- **Faith** also comes by hearing and hearing by the word of God (Romans 10:17).

- But let him ask **in faith**, nothing wavering, for he that wavereth is like a wave of the sea driven with the wind and tossed (James 1:6).

- Without **faith** it is impossible to please God (Hebrews 11:6).

- Things are moved by **faith** (Hebrews 11:33).

- Lack of **faith** can bring shipwreck (1Timothy1 18-19).

- If you have **faith** as a grain of mustard seed and say unto any mountain in your life, remove from here to there, it has to obey; and nothing shall be impossible unto you (Matthew 17:20).

- For whatsoever is born of God overcometh the world: and this is the victory that overcometh the world, even our **faith** (1 John 5:4).

FAITH IS THE KEY THAT PROCURES MIRACLES

When the disciples could not cast out the demon, it was a Faith issue: Matthew 17:16-20 *[16] And I brought him to thy disciples, and they could not cure him. [17] Then Jesus answered and said, O faithless and perverse generation, how long shall I be with you? how long shall I suffer you? bring him hither to me. [18] And Jesus rebuked the devil; and he departed out of him: and the child was cured from that very hour. [19] Then came the disciples to Jesus apart, and said, Why could not we cast him out? [20] And Jesus said unto them, Because of your unbelief: for verily I say unto you, If ye have faith as a grain of mustard seed, ye shall say unto this mountain, Remove hence to yonder place; and it shall remove; and nothing shall be impossible unto you.*

Jesus explains that it is essential to be strong in faith while praying, especially when confronting things that don't want to move and seem impossible to be moved. In addition, that these kinds of stubborn mountains (issues, demons, troubles) may require fasting and praying (Matthew 17:21).

When the Woman Touched the hem of Jesus'
garment, her deliverance came by faith and her
words: Matthew 9:20-22 [20] *And, behold, a woman, which*
was diseased with an issue of blood twelve years, came behind
him, and touched the hem of His garment: [21] *For she said within*
herself, If I may but touch His garment, I shall be whole.[22] *But*
Jesus turned him about, and when he saw her, he said, Daughter,
be of good comfort; thy faith hath made thee whole. And the
woman was made whole from that hour.

She approached the situation with faith,
determination and believing a miracle was possible.
Further enforcing mental and physical action with the
words she said to herself and reaching out to touch.
There is great healing, growth, and strength that comes
when we speak the right words in life and believe.

When the two blind men were healed, it was
according to their faith: Matthew 9:25-29 [25] *But when*
the people were put forth, he went in, and took her by the hand,
and the maid arose.26 And the fame hereof went abroad into all
that land.[27] *And when Jesus departed thence, two blind men*
followed him, crying, and saying, Thou son of David, have mercy
on us.[28] *And when he was come into the house, the blind men*

came to him: and Jesus saith unto them, Believe ye that I am able to do this? They said unto him, Yea, Lord.[29] Then touched he their eyes, saying, according to your faith be it unto you.

When they cried out to God they believed. They were desperate to receive healing and breakthrough and did not become ashamed or embarrassed to follow Jesus and cry out loud. Despite the judgment and criticism of others they remained persistence.

Regardless of our issues and in spite of the opinions of others, your desire to have an encounter with Jesus and be healed must outweigh everything else; surrender, cry loud and don't be ashamed! Let the sincerity of your heart and prayers grab God's attention.

JESUS LESSONS ON **FAITH: Matthew 21:18-21**

[18] Now in the morning as he returned into the city, he hungered. [19] And when he saw a fig tree in the way, he came to it, and found nothing thereon, but leaves only, and said unto it, Let no fruit grow on thee henceforward forever. And presently the fig tree withered away.[20] And when the disciples saw it, they marvelled, saying, How soon is the fig tree withered away![21] Jesus answered

and said unto them, Verily I say unto you, If ye have faith, and doubt not, ye shall not only do this which is done to the fig tree, but also if ye shall say unto this mountain, Be thou removed, and be thou cast into the sea; it shall be done.

When you know who lives on the inside of you and the power you carry, there is no reason to doubt. You would speak to every situation in your life and Keep your faith and trust in God. Anything blocking your ability to be fruitful must be destroyed and every mountain challenging your life must be cast in the sea.

Happy was Jesus to find a man of Faith. The centurion used faith and the word when asking of Jesus: Matt. 5-10 *[5] And when Jesus was entered into Capernaum, there came unto him a centurion, beseeching him, [6] And saying, Lord, my servant lieth at home sick of the palsy, grievously tormented. [7] And Jesus saith unto him, I will come and heal him. [8] The centurion answered and said, Lord, I am not worthy that thou shouldest come under my roof: but speak the word only, and my servant shall be healed. [9] For I am a man under authority, having soldiers under me: and I say to this man, Go, and he goeth; and to another, Come, and he cometh; and to* *my servant, Do this, and he doeth it. [10] When Jesus heard it, he marvelled, and said to them that followed, Verily I say unto you, I have not found so great faith, no, not in Israel.* **God is looking for His children to operate in confidence and unwavering belief. Trusting and believing without doubting.**

These aforementioned scriptures show, that it is faith and the word that moves God. For this reason, you should ask God to help you grow and increase in faith and in His word continuously. A little mustard seed grows into a tree. In like manner, your faith starting out small should become well-grounded, strong and unmovable in God. Growing from one level of faith to the next.

When you exercise your faith in a few things, it would become easier to utilize faith in all things, resulting in a strong trust relationship with God. Satan is always going to test your faith, but if you hold on to your faith regardless of what things look like with the physical eyes, he will never win!

THE WORD

- **The Word** is God, was always in the beginning with God and there was nothing made that was made without the Word. By **the word** was Jesus made flesh and became the **living word** (John 1).

- **The word** is also defined as the Sword of the Spirit (Ephesians 6:17) and is a shield (Prov. 30:5).

- Hebrews 4:12 states *"for **the word** of God is quick, and powerful, and sharper than any two-edged sword, piercing even to the dividing asunder of soul and spirit, and of the joints and marrow, and is a discerner of the thoughts and intents of the heart.* The Word of God Cuts!

- By **the Word** of God, we overcome the devil (1 John 2:14; Matt.4 1-11).

- Death and life is in the power of Spoken **Words** (the tongue-Proverbs 18:21).

- **The Word** of God is Spirit, Truth and Life changing.

As children of God, it has to be first nature to keep the Word of God in action through prayers. Furthermore, maintain a lifestyle of praying persistently, and keep an expectancy of answered prayers, deliverance, breakthroughs and change by praying.

When Jesus was tempted by Satan, He used the written Word to counteract against him (Matthew 4 1-11). We are taught to resist Satan and then he will flee (James 4); this is what Jesus did. He resisted Satan, rebuked Satan, bound and cast out devils, healed the sick and raised the dead.

You have two choices, either walk in faith or walk in fear! You have to have faith that God hears your prayers, answers prayers; that you will make it on top, accomplish your heart's desires, the goals you have for yourself; that your family will be saved with NO fear, only FAITH.

You have to guard your mind against doubt, unbelief, worry and let yet the inner drive of knowing that there is no failure in God and that He lives on the inside of you, keep you encouraged. God does not give His Children the spirit of fear but of Love, Power and of a Sound Mind and we as His children must be determined to walk in such.

God wants his children to have unshakable faith. It is only Satan that loves for the children of God to operate in the spirit of fear. He gets a kick out of operating in his mastership of lies and illusions that can create fear (John 8:44). He tries every trick he can to get the children of God to not operate in Faith and become driven by fear. For it is written in 2 Corinthians that Children of God must walk by faith and not by sight. This is the core principle we must live by.

Fear is a stronghold used by Satan to create worry and stress. Fear further stems other root causes of many sicknesses in the body, mentally, physically and spiritually; you can't even rest or sleep well with fear, doubt and worry. Satan wants to steal love, joy and peace and therefore fear has to be cast out of the mind immediately, before it grows deadly.

Proverbs 23 tells us that as a man thinks, so is he. Meaning you think happy; you feel good and happy. Think positive, you feel optimistic and content with a positive outlook on life. Think sad, you feel depressed, sad and hopeless. Romans 12:2 tells us that we can be transformed by the renewing of our mind. We must have the mind of

Christ.

Our mind and spiritual senses/feelings must be covered with the blood of Jesus and the helmet of salvation. The thoughts we entertain and what we believe about ourselves, will produce our success or failure in life. It is important to not be a caged son/daughter of God.

We cannot put limits on what God can do in our life if we let him. We cannot also limit how we operate in faith. God has great deliverance, wisdom, teaching, understanding, healing, salvation, redemption and restorative power to move in our lives.

Part of the spiritual armor gear God has given us, includes the helmet of salvation. The helmet of salvation covers your mind, thoughts and is near to your eyes (spiritual sight), ears (spiritual hearing), nose (spiritual smell), mouth (words); all connected and processed through the brain/mind.

If this area is left vulnerable, the enemy will create strategies to impact the mind and invade your thoughts with negativity. You must shield your mind with the light and word of God. Always cover your mind!

The enemy will use any part of your body to attack

and enter through by whatever means: the eyes, ears, appetite, taste, smell and touch, if you allow him; we have to protect our gates at all times. Renewing your mind and wearing the helmet goes hand and hand. You have to keep your mind renewed daily with the word of God and walk in the shoes of a child of God; you do not have to be afraid to do so.

In life we are going to experience good times and many challenging times. But during the bad times you cannot have the mind of a son or daughter of God, walking around in pity feeling defeated and hopeless in a battle or storm, when God has already defeated Satan; you must fight the good fight of faith, because it's not the other way around; God has won the victory, so have you, if you believe.

It is God who created all things including Satan. Satan was cast out of Heaven because of his rebellion and has no power over God and only has power in our lives if we don't evict him out of it and restrict his access from reentering. God who dwells on the inside of His children is greater than any issue, obstacle, challenge or battle. Struggling in a battle when God has already provided us with victory through Christ

Jesus, is unnecessary.

We are taught by the Holy Spirit that we are supposed to speak the word of God to the situations that present themselves in our life. Everything must hear your words! Speak the word, pray, keep faith and wait on God's timing. It is during this process we are developed and taught by God, and our trust grows.

Therefore, by the word of God, any mountain, problem, mulberry tree in our path should not see you, but God the Father, the Son Jesus Christ and the Holy Spirit, that dwells on the inside of you, "Not you". It is God that fights and defends when we pray, ask and speak His word. What can stand up against God and win? Don't be afraid to trust God. Have faith and trust in God! When challenges come, keep your faith and keep your joy.

The Enemy loves to steal our joy in effort to bring weakness. It is the joy of the Lord that's our strength (so worship and praise). If you make it a pattern to pray the word, to dance, worship, sing and stomp on the devil's head, in the mist of even Hell, you will be in peace in the mist of Hell.

The Devil would find it challenging to manipulate your life, emotions, thoughts, feelings and mind. He will not be successful at all because he would not be able to steal your joy, faith, trust and the word. You will have the victory constantly, if you block him from manipulating and controlling your emotions and impulses on how you react. When things happen *pray quickly*, letting prayer be your automatic first response.

Always keep a praise, no matter the time or challenge. Praise and worship more when challenges and storms come. It will create a protective atmosphere and repeal and/or break yokes and bring quick results of victory. Worship the Lord our God who has the power to change everything!

How do you define faith? What can you do to better walk in faith? What does the Word of God mean to you? What can you do to better apply the Word of God in your life and not take it for granted?

_____
_____
_____
_____
_____
_____
_____
_____
_____
_____
_____
_____
_____
_____
_____
_____
_____
_____
_____
_____
_____
_____
_____
_____
_____
_____
_____
_____

Chapter Four
Applying Wisdom

Without knowledge, wisdom and understanding of who you are as a child of God, knowing the tools available to you at hand and how to use them, can do nothing but lead you to fail! Again, the enemy advantage and our weakness, is ignorance. God wants His children to seek perfect wisdom from above.

Without having the knowledge and instructions God wants us to have, we become vulnerable ignorant children, with a life full of turmoil, all because we fail to know lifesaving information. It is priority to know the truth about Jesus Christ and who you are in Him before you can be free. There is nothing vulnerable or ignorant about God and we as

His children should line up with His characteristics. It is important to read your Bible, know the word of God by studying and ask guidance from the Holy Spirit; doing it all with faith.

God wants us to seek knowledge, wisdom and understanding and use it wisely in everything at all times. Lack of these attributes can really kill us and make life hard. The type of wisdom you have can determine your life or death.

If you don't know you're allergic to shell fish and eat it, what can happen? But if you have this information and understanding, would you still eat it? We must be equipped and well established to operate effectively as a child of God. Not having proper data can be harmful but the right information can protect and take you far in life.

Lack of knowledge can bring many problems and hardships, when you should be walking in blessings, prosperity and victory. Wisdom allows one to have an advantage in make good choices and decisions in life. The only way for the enemy to not have an advantage in our lives is for us to use Godly wisdom (2 Corinthians 2:11). The enemy is happy when children of God are unaware of the authority and rights they have. This gives him opportunity to easily steal assets that rightfully belongs to you.

What you do not know you cannot wisely enforce, seek, request or receive. When you embrace wisdom, you are walking in the light of God, but without it there is only darkness. You cannot see clearly in the dark. Walk in who you are; as a child of light you must walk in light, as the head and not the tail. Proverbs tells us that wisdom is more valuable that silver, gold and rubies and only fools will reject wisdom. Wisdom is the principle that supports knowledge, understanding, good health, long life, right relationships, decision making and a prosperous life; money cannot buy you these things.

SCRIPTURES ON WISDOM:

James 1:5- ⁵ *If any of you lack wisdom, let him ask of God, that giveth to all men liberally, and upbraideth not; and it shall be given him.*

Proverbs 1:7 *⁷The fear of the Lord is the beginning of knowledge; fools despise wisdom and instruction.*

Proverbs 2:6-8 *⁶For the Lord gives wisdom; from His mouth comes knowledge and understanding; ⁷he stores up sound wisdom for the upright;*

he is a shield to those who walk in integrity. *⁸Guarding the paths of the justice and watching over the way of the saints. ⁹Then you will understand righteousness and justice and equity, every good path; ¹⁰for wisdom will come into your heart and knowledge will be pleasant to your soul; ¹¹discretion will guard you, ¹²delivering you from the way of evil, from men of perverted speech,*

James 3:17 *¹⁷ But the wisdom that is from above is first pure, then peaceable, gentle, and easy to be intreated, full of mercy and good fruits, without partiality, and without hypocrisy.*

Proverbs 3:13-18 *¹³ Happy is the man that findeth wisdom, and the man that getteth understanding.¹⁴ For the merchandise of it is better than the merchandise of silver, and the gain thereof than fine gold.¹⁵ She is more precious than rubies: and all the things thou canst desire are not to be compared unto her.¹⁶ Length of days is in her right hand; and in her left hand riches and honour.¹⁷ Her ways are ways of pleasantness, and all her paths are peace.¹⁸ She is a tree of life to them that lay hold upon her: and happy is every one that retaineth her.*

Proverbs 4:5-9 *⁵Get wisdom, get understanding: forget it not; neither decline from the words of my mouth.6 Forsake her not, and she shall* *preserve thee: love her, and she shall keep thee.[7] Wisdom is the principal thing; therefore get wisdom: and with all thy getting get understanding.[8] Exalt her, and she shall promote thee: she shall bring thee to honour, when thou dost embrace her.[9] She shall give to thine head an ornament of grace: a crown of glory shall she deliver to thee.*

Proverbs 16: 16 [16] *How much better is it to get wisdom than gold! and to get understanding rather to be chosen than silver!*

Proverbs 24:14 - [14] *So shall the knowledge of wisdom be unto thy soul: when thou hast found it, then there shall be a reward, and thy expectation shall not be cut off.*

1 King 3:9- [9] *Give therefore thy servant an understanding heart to judge thy people, that I may discern between good and bad: for who is able to judge this thy so great a people.*

SCRIPTURES ON APPLYING WISDOM:

Deuteronomy 28: 1-14 - *And it shall come to pass, if thou shalt hearken diligently unto the voice of the Lord thy God, to observe and to do all his commandments which I command thee this day, that the Lord thy God will set thee on high above all nations of the earth:[2] And all these* *blessings shall come on thee, and overtake thee, if thou shalt hearken unto the voice of the Lord thy God.[3] Blessed shalt thou be in the city, and blessed shalt thou be in the field.[4] Blessed shall be the fruit of thy body, and the fruit of thy ground, and the fruit of thy cattle, the increase of thy kine, and the flocks of thy sheep.[5] Blessed shall be thy basket and thy store.[6] Blessed shalt thou be when thou comest in, and blessed shalt thou be when thou goest out. [7] The Lord shall cause thine enemies that rise up against thee to be smitten before thy face: they shall come out against thee one way, and flee before thee seven ways.[8] The Lord shall command the blessing upon thee in thy storehouses, and in all that thou settest thine hand unto; and he shall bless thee in the land which the Lord thy God giveth thee.[9] The Lord shall establish thee an holy people unto himself, as he hath sworn unto thee, if thou shalt keep the commandments of the Lord thy God, and walk in his ways.[10] And all people of the earth shall see that thou art called by the name of the Lord; and they shall be afraid of thee.[11] And the Lord shall make thee plenteous in goods, in the fruit of thy body, and in the fruit of thy cattle, and in the fruit of thy ground, in the land which the Lord sware unto thy fathers to give thee.[12] The Lord shall open unto thee His good treasure, the heaven to give the rain unto thy land in His season, and to bless all the work of thine hand: and thou shalt lend unto many nations, [13] And the Lord shall make thee the head, and not the tail; and thou shalt be above only, and thou shalt not be* beneath; if that thou hearken unto the commandments of the Lord thy God, which I command thee this day, to observe and to do them:[14] And thou shalt not go aside from any of the words which I command thee this day, to the right hand, or to the left, to go after other gods to serve them.

Exodus 15:26 - [26] And said, If thou wilt diligently hearken to the voice of the Lord thy God, and wilt do that which is right in his sight, and wilt give ear to his commandments, and keep all his statutes, I will put none of these diseases upon thee, which I have brought upon the Egyptians: for I am the Lord that healeth thee.

Deuteronomy 30:19-20 - [19] I call heaven and earth to record this day against you, that I have set before you life and death, blessing and cursing: therefore choose life, that both thou and thy seed may live: [20] That thou mayest love the Lord thy God, and that thou mayest obey his voice, and that thou mayest cleave unto him: for he is thy life, and the length of thy days: that thou mayest dwell in the land which the Lord sware unto thy fathers, to Abraham, to Isaac, and to Jacob, to give them.

Isaiah 40:28-31 - [28] Hast thou not known? hast thou not heard, that the everlasting God, the Lord, the Creator of the ends of the earth, fainteth not, neither is weary? there is no searching of his *understanding.*[29] *He giveth power to the faint; and to them that have no might he increase strength.*[30] *Even the youths shall faint and be weary, and the young men shall utterly fall:*[31] *But they that wait upon the Lord shall renew their strength; they shall mount up with wings as eagles; they shall run, and not be weary; and they shall walk, and not faint.*

WISDOM IS AN IMPORTANT ASSET

❖ It allows you to apply knowledge

❖ Helps you maintain self-control

❖ Understand the importance of a disciplined

life

❖ Make you yield towards good choices

❖ Gives you an advantage

❖ Permits you to make well informed decisions

❖ Can save your life

❖ Minimizes unnecessary hardships

❖ Eliminates struggles

❖ Leads to spiritual, physical, emotional and

financial wealth

❖ Brings joy and happiness

❖ Necessary to walk in prosperity

❖ Prevents turmoil

❖ Packaged with blessings that overflow

.

SELF REFLECTIONS YOU MAY WANT TO JOURNAL

What is wisdom? Why is it essential for your spiritual growth? How can you seek wisdom from God?

_____

_____

_____

_____

_____

_____

_____

_____

_____

_____

_____

_____

_____

_____

_____

_____

_____

_____

_____

_____

_____

_____

_____

_____

_____

_____

_____

_____

_____

_____

Chapter Five
Power of Prayer

Prayer is our communication with God. In communication one listens and another speaks. For this reason, it is beneficial to practice being still (silent/quiet) after reading (studying) and praying, so you can hear God speak.

Prayer is a powerful key tool in our walk as children of God; even Jesus lived a life of prayer. So, if Jesus the Son of the Living God lived a lifestyle of prayer, what about us? In John the 17th chapters 1-26 it further shows how Jesus prayed to the Father for us.

Jesus also encouraged us to have a prayer life. In addition, to loving our enemies and praying for those who persecute us, He also gave us instructions on how to pray (Matt. 5:44; Matt 6:1-15). Prayer enforces things and situations to shift on your behalf. It is God's will for you to be delivered and not bound by any weight from the challenges of life. Prayer is a tool that pulls you from the flesh into the spirit. Disconnecting you from the negative forces and emotions that can manipulate your peace.

In other words, it allows you to be released from heaviness, burdens, depression, anxiety, fear and other stuff that strongholds bring to keep you from moving forward (1 Thessalonians 5: 17-18; Hebrews 12:1).

Mark 1:34-35 *34 And he healed many that were sick of divers diseases, and cast out many devils; and suffered not the devils to speak, because they knew him. 35 And in the morning, rising up a great while before day, he went out, and departed into a solitary place, and there prayed.*

Matthew 11:25-26 *25 At that time Jesus answered and said, I thank thee, O Father, Lord of heaven and earth, because thou hast hid these things from the wise and prudent, and hast revealed them unto babes. 26 Even so, Father: for so it seemed good in thy sight.*

Luke 6:12 *And it came to pass in those days, that he went out into a mountain to pray, and continued all night in prayer to God.*

Luke 22:41-44 *[41] And he was withdrawn from them about a stone's cast, and kneeled down, and prayed, [42] Saying, Father, if thou be willing, remove this cup from me: nevertheless not my will, but thine, be done. [43] And there appeared an angel unto him from heaven, strengthening him. [44] And being in an agony he prayed more earnestly: and his sweat was as it were great drops of blood falling down to the ground.*

Luke 23:34 *[34] Then said Jesus, Father, forgive them; for they know not what they do. And they parted his raiment, and cast lots.*

John 11: 41-42 *[41] Then they took away the stone from the place where the dead was laid. And Jesus lifted up his eyes, and said, Father, I thank thee that thou hast heard me. [42] And I knew that thou hearest me always: but because of the people which stand by I said it, that they may believe that thou hast sent me.*

John 12-27-28 *²⁷ Now is my soul troubled; and what shall I say? Father, save me from this hour: but for this cause came I unto this hour.²⁸ Father, glorify thy name. Then came there a voice from heaven, saying, I have both glorified it, and will glorify it again.*

Hebrews 5:7 *⁷ Who in the days of his flesh, when he had offered up prayers and supplications with strong crying and tears unto him that was able to save him from death, and was heard in that he feared;*

SCRIPTURES ON PRAYER:

1 Peter 3:12 For *the eyes of the Lord are over the righteous, and his ears are open unto their prayers: but the face of the Lord is against them that do evil.*

1 Corinthians 14:15 What *is it then? I will pray with the spirit, and I will pray with the understanding also: I will sing with the spirit, and I will sing with the understanding also.*

Psalms 55:17 *Evening, and morning, and at noon, will I pray, and cry aloud: and He shall hear my voice.*

Matthew 26:41 *Watch and pray, that ye enter not into temptation: the spirit indeed is willing, but the flesh is weak.*

James 5:16 *Confess your faults one to another, and pray one for another, that ye may be healed. The effectual fervent prayer of a righteous man availeth much.*

1 Corinthians 7:5 *Defraud ye not one the other, except it be with consent for a time, that ye may give yourselves to fasting and prayer; and come together again, that Satan tempt you not for your incontinency.*

Luke 18:1 And *he spake a parable unto them to this end, that men ought always to pray, and not to faint.*

John 16: 20-13 Verily, *verily, I say unto you, That ye shall weep and lament, but the world shall rejoice: and ye shall be sorrowful, but your sorrow shall be turned into joy.* ^{21} *A woman when she is in travail hath sorrow, because her hour is come: but as soon as she is delivered of the child,   she remembereth no more the anguish, for joy that a man is born into the world.* ^{22} *And ye now therefore have sorrow: but I will see you again, and your heart shall rejoice, and your joy no man taketh from you.* ^{23}

And in that day ye shall ask me nothing. Verily, verily, I say unto you, Whatsoever ye shall ask the Father in my name, he will give it you.

John 15:7 *If ye abide in me, and my words abide in you, ye shall ask what ye will, and it shall be done unto you.*

Philippians 4:6 *Be careful for nothing; but in everything by prayer and supplication with thanksgiving let your requests be made known unto God.*

Mark 11:24 *Therefore I say unto you, what things soever ye desire, when ye pray, believe that ye receive them, and ye shall have [them].*

1 Thessalonians 5:17 Pray *without ceasing.*

Matthew 6:7 But *when ye pray, use not vain repetitions, as the heathen do: for they think that they shall be heard for their much speaking.*

Luke 11:9 *And I say unto you, Ask, and it shall be given you; seek, and ye shall find; knock, and it shall be opened unto* *you.*

Romans 8:26 *Likewise the Spirit also helpeth our infirmities: for we know not what we should pray for as we ought: but the Spirit itself maketh intercession for us with groanings which cannot be uttered.*

Matthew 6:6 *But thou, when thou prayest, enter into thy closet, and when thou hast shut thy door, pray to thy Father which is in secret; and thy Father which seeth in secret shall reward thee openly.*

1 Timothy 2: 1 *I exhort therefore, that, first of all, supplications, prayers, intercessions, [and] giving of thanks, be made for all men;*

Jeremiah 33:3 *Call unto me, and I will answer thee, and shew thee great and mighty things, which thou knowest not.*

Ephesians 6:18 *Praying always with all prayer and supplication in the Spirit, and watching thereunto with all perseverance and*
supplication for all saints;

Psalms 34:17 *The righteous cry, and the LORD heareth, and delivereth them out of all their troubles.*

Colossians 4:2 Continue *in prayer, and watch in the same with thanksgiving;*

Matthew 6:5-8 *And when thou prayest, thou shalt not be as the hypocrites [are]: for they love to pray standing in the synagogues and in the corners of the streets, that they may be seen of men. Verily I say unto you, They have their reward.*

Matthew 6:9 *After this manner therefore pray ye: Our Father which art in heaven, Hallowed be thy name.*

Matthew 6:1-34 - *Take heed that ye do not your alms before men, to be seen of them: otherwise ye have no reward of your Father which is in heaven.*

Prayer is personal and intimate communication with God. It's an extremely valuable principle that aids children of God in having a strong spiritual life. That is why children of God are advised to always pray and not faint (Luke 18:1).

Prayer helps to build our Faith and Trust in God. Just like you want to have trust in God, God wants children that He can trust also; trusting in Him at all times (Psalms 62:8). Mature children that have developed into having the mind of Christ, who think like Christ, pray like Christ, have faith like Christ and apply the language of Christ; who are strong in the Lord and in the power of his might!

This comes with knowledge, wisdom, and understanding from the Holy Spirit. Children of God should practice the application of Jesus Christ teachings and principles as a daily way of life, not like an off and on switch; it should be a continuous way of life. When you sincerely seek God, love him and desire to make him smile upon you, you humbly fear him. It is also this fear that will keep you from sinning, if you want to be kept.

Remember the fear of the Lord is the beginning of wisdom (Proverbs 9:10; Psalms 111:10). Studying, meditating and knowing the Word of God allows one to understand the requirements for receiving the promises of God and how to develop a strong prayer language. So, knowing the Word of God goes right alongside with prayer.

In prayer, it is good to apply scripture prayer points, along with the promise of God, to enforce the manifestation of the Word and to demonstrate to the enemy that you are aware of His position and yours. His place is under your feet and your position is to recognize what Jesus did on the cross, who you are as a child of God and know the spiritual principles to receive the blessing of the Lord; that make you rich spiritually, emotionally, physically, mentally and adds no sorrow (Proverb 10:22).

Therefore, enforcing your authority by "rebuking" Satan and "binding up" any demonic and wicked force trying to operate in your life to bring destruction, aggravation, irritations, conflict, and sickness, is your given right. Luke 10 tells and shows that God has given His children all power over Satan and demonic forces that come against us.

If you operate in fear, you would be a joke to Satan and His demons and they will not take what you try to enforce seriously and frequently test you. When you fear, you give them access and permission to ignore your commands because they are connected to the spirit of fear. You cannot walk in fear and trust at the same time; you have to choose.

Please remember Satan cannot be bound up, God gave him permission to move To and Fro on the earth (Job 1:7; 1 Peter 5:8). You have to rebuke and resist Satan and then he will flee. Demons and ill spoken words you can bind. A lot can be done through prayer. The armor of God (Ephesians 6) cannot even be put on without prayer nor can it be applied without faith.

Prayer is more than just communication, it's a tool we use to enforce our rights through Jesus Christ when binding, loosing, decreeing, declaring, placing angels on assignment, renouncing, restricting access and giving commands. The application of prayer helps us in every area of our life.

It is an essential weapon and remedy used to address every trouble, issue and situation in our life (James 5:13); everything can be addressed by praying. Praying persistently, strongly and sincerely in all matters of our life should be a daily routine at least three times a day or more (Psalms 55:17; Luke 18:1; 1 Thess. 5:17; Ephesians 6:18; Joshua 1:8). In all keep faith in God. He does not want our faith to fail (Luke

22:32)!

Truth is, it wasn't until I got to the point of being tired of the Devil constantly attacking me and my children that I began to pray like my life depended on it, because actually it did. I knew God, so I couldn't entertain killing myself as an option; on the other hand, I decided if I had to fight I would. I declared I would fight the good fight and not go down easily.

I decided that I would no longer complain if I had to go through the fire. As long as God was with me, I would just go through. Hoping too, that my challenging experiences were not in vain but could be used to help someone else. It once seemed like the pain in my life out weighted any good but when I turned my life into constant prayers, I became a renewed person, strong in the Lord.

I had to go through many lessons repeatedly until I passed the test and learned the significance of completely surrendering my life to God and developing a strong prayer life. I no longer waited for the enemy to attack; I became proactive with prevention.

By placing restrictions on demonic access in my

life and commanding every evil force, deaf, dumb, mute and confused back to the demonic world (hell) and/or to be destroyed by the Fire of God, I learned to spiritually block potential attacks before they can even touch my life physically.

The enemy was served that he has been evicted from my house, health, children, purpose, destiny, future, career, finances, possessions and anyone or thing connected to me. Prayer has become a strong part of my daily routine; I am never too tired to pray and I love to pray more now than I ever did in the past.

When I started to embrace a life strongly center by prayer, my life went through a transformation of great change quickly. So, what I share in this book is not just the truth, it's my experience and testimony. I don't share my whole story in this book but what I will add is, I went through first class hell and it was only the Lords doing that bought me out victoriously with the ability to set others free.

Prayer is essential but without faith, will not be effective. What do you have to lose by believing? The teaching of Jesus showed that breakthrough, healing and deliverance is according to one's faith. You can only truly face your fears and the Devil with faith.

Satan will try diligently to scare you, but you must not be moved and never let lose your faith and trust in God. As you pass even this test you will make elevation to the next level and lesson.

In addition, I strongly believe that God wants His son and daughters to see him deeper than just for the benefits that come along with serving Him. He is more than our healer, He is more than the miracles, more than receiving, breakthroughs, deliverance, wealth and prosperity, He is our everything! He is our God, our father and creator; the breath we take and the food we eat; He loves us.

He wants us to Love Him for who He is and He is God all by Himself. He wants us to seek intimacy with Him, to go where He is our first Love. Daily we can desire to please Him, make Him happy and put a smile upon His face; knowing what His plans are for our lives.

To build a relationship with Him on a level that shows we trust and totally and completely have faith in Him to be El Shaddai in our lives. This extends to the point where when we pray, we are not afraid because we have faith that our God will work out the situation and settle every matter and where entertaining fear and doubt is extinguished from our walk because our faith is so strong.

He loves us so much that He did not even want sin to separate us from Him. His love runs so deep and wide that no man can measure it. He made us in His image and likeness. Even when Adam's disobedience "created sin and death" that separated and took us from the presence of God, Our Heavenly Father sent Jesus to redeem us, so that we will have "life" and have it more abundantly; in lieu of death. Allowing us the opportunity to return back into God's presence, the way it was initially intended before Adam Sinned (John 3:16; John 14:23); this is love.

That is also why there is no more condemnations for those (His Children) who are in Christ Jesus. We mean more to God than our sins, short comings and/or faults. Some things you just have to shake off, hold your head up, forgive yourself or someone else if required, and try again. There is nothing we can do to stop God from loving us. Even those who are living in darkness He loves, regardless of whether they know it or care. He loves His creations and for this reason, the sun shines on the just as well as the unjust (Matthew 5:45).

In this, when we should strongly seek to live a life pleasing to God. In addition to avoid intentionally doing anything that will displease Him. He does not want us to take advantage of His love and keep using His grace as a scapegoat, to keep backsliding and falling into repeating cycles of sin.

When you pray, know that God loves you so much that He hears your prayers. With this insight, you can pray sincerely in faith, knowing that He wants to answer your prayers. Be humble and patient and do not demand on timing or how and when He should move. Let God Be God and demonstrate how He moves! Pray and worship while you wait. Do it all in faith!

Ask God for the grace to have the spirit to pray and worship daily. Don't be intimidated by what some situations may look like, just speak the word of God to it and let God fight for you, rather than fighting for yourself. Let your actions reveal that the situations have no power to manipulate your joy, control over your faith or peace of mind. Don't give the devil your power.

The more things look rough, let your prayers go deeper, stronger and longer. Fight the good fight of faith and once you put a situation in God's hand, leave it there and don't take it out! As long as you allow God to be the head over your life, he will be, but if you take it out of his hands then he will wait. It is easy to rejoice during good times but not so easy when times are hard. I wrote this book hoping that you would be encouraged and develop a stronger trust and faith in God. I pray your trust in God will no longer be controlled by challenging times.

I pray that your faith and prayer life will be persistent at all times, to see the revelation why the Apostle Paul said to find it all joy when you go through (James 1). You will come out stronger and wiser, with faith and trust that has grown into maturity.

Don't allow your mind, faith, belief, hope, love, life, destiny, purpose or future to be *caged by fear*, the opposite of faith. Fear brings limitation and stagnation to your life. If your mind is overtaken by the enemy your life becomes in jeopardy physically and spiritually.

Therefore, it is critical to keep the helmet of salvation on at all times. If your head is left vulnerable and becomes injured, physically or spiritually, you can encounter a battle with physical or spiritual death. Do not allow your mind to be cage nor put how God operate in a cage. Protect your mind with the word of God.

Pray your way through every situation strongly and sincerely in faith. Don't be a scared and weak-minded believer! Seek and pray to God, for He is a rewarder of those that diligently seek Him. Don't be discouraged because of trials and tribulations, you will always have them; exercise your faith. In God, you will always overcome them. Break free into God's purpose for your life by keeping your faith and trust in God no matter what. Practice walking in the confidence of that. He desires above all things that you prosper and be in good health in every area of your life; Trust God! Have Faith!

SELF REFLECTIONS YOU MAY WANT TO JOURNAL

How do you define prayer? Do you feel encouraged to pray more from what your read so far? If so, what can you do to increase your prayer life?

_____

_____

_____

_____

_____

_____

_____

_____

_____

_____

_____

_____

_____

_____

_____

_____

_____

_____

_____

_____

_____

_____

_____

_____

_____

_____

_____

_____

_____

Chapter Six
Valuable Lessons

Deuteronomy 7:9-9 *Know therefore that the Lord thy God, he is God, the faithful God, which keepeth covenant and mercy with them that love him and keep his commandments to a thousand generations;* **You must know God is Faithful; establish a relationship upon the foundation of trust so that you may walk by faith at all times.**

Ephesians 6:12 - *For we wrestle not against flesh and blood, but against principalities, against powers, against the rulers of the darkness of this world, against spiritual wickedness in high places.* **You must know that your fight is a spiritual fight, not with man but the spirit behind the man and the Spirit behind the situation.**

Ephesians 6:11 - *Put on the whole armor of God, that ye may be able to stand against the wiles of the devil.* **The armor of God is your defense strategy against the Enemy wicked agenda and tactics (above all faith is the most essential). Ware the armor in faith, confidence and trust, that God has equipped you for spiritual warfare with the proper defense weapons.**

2 Corinthians 10:3-6 - *For though we walk in the flesh, we do not war after the flesh: [4] (For the weapons of our warfare are not carnal, but mighty through God to the pulling down of strong holds;) [5] Casting down imaginations, and every high thing that exalteth itself against the knowledge of God, and bringing into captivity every thought to the obedience of Christ;* **You have to reject the voice of enemy and renounce thoughts (doubt, fear, depression, anxiety, worry) that do not line up with the word of God. You must cast it all down. Then speak the word of God against every bad thought. Take authority by the power of God, the Son Jesus Christ and the Holy spirit, and command mental conflict and chatter to cease immediately.**

Exercise your mental faith, your mind will not be in a

cage and you will not live in a mental prison! Renew you mind by the word of God, decree the mind of Christ, and worship. keep a song and praise in your heart because God keep those in perfect peace who mind is stayed on Him.

Psalms 91:1 - *He that dwelleth in the secret place of the most High shall abide under the shadow of the Almighty.* **The children of God dwell in the safety and protection of God, He is our refuge and present help.**

1 Peter 5:8 - *Be sober, be vigilant; because your adversary the devil, as a roaring lion, walketh about, seeking whom he may devour:* **You must not sleep on the enemy and constantly be wise of his devices; this comes with paying attention. He will use any means to attack your joy and peace and sneak upon you most, when you appear to be weak and vulnerable. We should bless the Lord at all times. When you are going through challenging times, constant praise, worship and prayer will confuse the enemy and make you unpredictable.**

James 4:7 - *Submit yourselves therefore to God. Resist the devil, and* *he will flee from you.* **Guard you mind, resist and shun evil. Have a spirit that love what God loves and hate what God hates. By all means never yield to sin/temptation.**

Ephesians 6:13 - *Wherefore take unto you the whole armor of God, that ye may be able to withstand in the evil day, and having done all, to stand.* **Wearing the armor properly mentally, spiritually and in daily life application, allows you to always come out the battle a winner. The victory was already won, you just have to stand your ground on the word and faith; it is for your protection.**

Deuteronomy 28:7 - *The LORD shall cause thine enemies that rise up against thee to be smitten before thy face: they shall come out against thee one way, and flee before thee seven ways.* **The Lord will fight against every force that comes up against you, if you allow him. A simple prayer: "Lord fight for me!" don't have to say much, just ask the lord to fight your battle (Exodus 14:14).**

Luke 10:19 - *Behold, I give unto you power to tread on serpents and scorpions, and over all the power of the enemy: and nothing shall by any means hurt you.* **If the Spirit of God and his word**

dwells on the inside of you, no demon can stand up against God and win, therefore do not be afraid and remember nothing can harm you so don't entertain otherwise. God did not give the enemy power over you. He gave you power over the enemy.

Victory was given to you, therefore keep your mind anchored in God and the Word. Every stronghold and force trying to hold you back and create problems in your: mind, body, spirit, soul, health, family, children, destiny, career and future, will have to let you lose when you exercise this authority.

2 Corinthians 11:14 - *And no marvel; for Satan himself is transformed into an angel of light.* Satan is a master of lies and illusions. He operates on what the natural eyes can see in efforts to manipulate children of God. This is why we are not supposed to be moved by what things look like (the physical eyes can see), for we are supposed to walk by faith and not by sight. Therefore, we must not be shaken or moved from our position based on what things "appear" to be. Remember what is seen physically is not really the final outcome and how you move determines

Satan's advantage over you.

1 John 5:4-5 - *For whatsoever is born of God overcometh the world: and this is the victory that overcometh the world, [even] our faith.* **You must know you are an 'over comer' through Christ Jesus. Greater is he that lives on the inside of you than he that lives in the world. Let God arise and fear be scattered!**

1 Corinthians 10:4 - *For the weapons of our warfare are not carnal, but mighty through God to the pulling down of strong holds.* **Our spiritual weapons are more than enough to destroy strongholds.**

Matthew 18:18-20 - *Verily I say unto you, Whatsoever ye shall bind on earth shall be bound in heaven: and whatsoever ye shall loose on earth shall be loosed in heaven.* **You have power to loose and to bind demons and their powers. Heaven will agree with you when you operate this authority on earth-Thy kingdom come they will be done on earth as it is in heaven.**

Ephesians 6:13-18 - *13 Wherefore take unto you the whole armor of God, that ye may be able to withstand in the evil day, and having done all, to stand. 14 Stand therefore, having your loins girt about with truth, and having on the breastplate of righteousness; 15 And your feet shod* *with the preparation of the gospel of peace;16 Above all, taking the shield of faith, wherewith ye shall be able to quench all the fiery darts of the wicked.17 And take the helmet of salvation, and the sword of the Spirit, which is the word of God:18 Praying always with all prayer and supplication in the Spirit, and watching thereunto with all perseverance and supplication for all saints.* We must be dressed properly in our spiritual armor. We cannot be half dressed. Having on the armor requires constant practice for the development of confidence and faith that you are able to apply the appropriate fighting strategies and weaponry, based on the type of fight, storm or attack. Therefore, mental attitude, knowledge, wisdom and understanding of your resources and studying how the enemy operates allows you to be a spiritually equipped soldier in the army of God. You have to take on the mind and confidence of a well-trained soldier. If you don't have faith and confidence, you cannot properly wear the armor well nor be able to use the spiritual weaponry without being afraid. Without faith you will lose the fight. Above all you must have faith! Faith is a powerful force in which God made and framed the world. Also, we are saved by faith, it goes along with the word, the main ingredient for which we live.

SELF REFLECTIONS YOU MAY WANT TO JOURNAL

Writes down your notes and thoughts.

_____
_____
_____
_____
_____
_____
_____
_____
_____
_____
_____
_____
_____
_____
_____
_____
_____
_____
_____
_____
_____
_____
_____
_____
_____
_____
_____
_____
_____
_____
_____

Be careful for nothing; but in everything by prayer and supplication with thanksgiving let your requests be made known unto God. And the peace of God, which passeth all understanding, shall keep your hearts and minds through Christ Jesus.

Philippians 4:6-7

Chapter Seven

Prayers

At this point in the Book, your mind should be renewed on who you are as a Child of God and Spirit ready to be transformed and operate into purpose. Now let's pray with our mind focused strongly on God and in Faith. Let's destroy every cage of fear, doubt, inadequacy, setback and failure through faith, the word of God and powerful prayers.

Below are some prayers you can use as a guide with your own prayers. Pray strong, intentional and expecting a great outcome that God will perfect everything concerning your life. That He will help you to be and become who He created you to be, before the foundation of the world, before you were formed in your mother's womb.

Prayer One

Dear Father,

I come before you repenting of my sins. Asking you to forgive me for anything that I have done wrong intentionally or unintentionally. I also choose to forgive those who have offended and trespassed against me; I lay what was done at your feet that you may move in a manner that you see fit.

I ask that you take total control of my life today. I decree and declare I walk in a higher level of Faith today than I did yesterday; I grow and develop daily in you. Father I ask that you guide and direct my path, decisions and choices, for you know what is best for me. I decree and declare that your will is my will and my will your will.

Renew my mind and order my steps today. Renew my mind in your word & saturate my mind, body and spirit in your word. That I may pray as your child, think as your child today, speak as your child today, operate as your child today, have faith as your child today, take authority as your child today.

That I may not be moved by sight nor be afraid of the terror by night nor the arrows that fly by day. I will not be shaken/moved by the enemy's lies, schemes and tactics. You have not given me the spirit of Fear but of love, power and a sound mind. Therefore, I decree and declare that I walk in the Spirit of Love, I walk in the Spirit of Power and the Spirit of a Sound mind.

I cover my mind in the Blood of Jesus. I cover my hands, body, spirit and soul in the Blood of Jesus. My goals, dreams, destiny, career and purpose in the blood of Jesus. I cover my family, children, friendships, home and work environment in the blood of Jesus. My traveling of me and my family and all my possessions, in the Blood of Jesus.

In the name of Jesus, I block and cancel every wicked assignment of the enemy concerning my life, children and family and anything connected to me today. Whatever methods Satan uses in an attempt to bring aggregation, irritations, confusion, chaos, hardships or fear in my life, I cancel it and deny it access to interrupt my life.

I decree and declare it shall not prosper, for my eyes are shielded in faith. I uproot and cast every demonic seed the enemy planted in my mind, spirit and body while I was sleeping into the fire of God to be destroyed. I command Every demonic implant be uprooted and cast into the fire, now in the name of Jesus Christ.

I rebuke sickness, illness, disease and afflictions, I command it out of my body and life. In the name of Jesus, I speak that I shall prosper and be in good health in every area of my life! I decree and declare that I am free from all curses, witchcraft powers, yokes and strongholds in the name of Jesus! I destroy every wall, blockage, cage and box impacting my mind, life, liberations, abundance, family, children, health, career, relationships, finances, destiny, purpose and future.

I can do all things through Christ Jesus who strengthens me. Therefore, in the name of Jesus I shall not be stuck, I shall not be blocked in anyway but I will move forward and advance in Jesus' name!

Jesus came that I may have life and have it more abundantly. I decree and declare an abundant life in Jesus' name. I shall prosper in the Lord, advance and have great success in Jesus' name. It cannot be otherwise!

Prayer Two (Luke 3 and Matthew 13)

In the Name of Jesus, Angels of the Lord, prepare ye the way of the Lord in my life. Make His path straight in my life! Let every valley be filled and every valley and hill be brought low and the crooked ways made straight, the rough ways made smooth and let all see the salvation of God the Father who is in Heaven.

Uproot every weed that the enemy has sowed into my body, mind, life, family, children finances, relationships while I was sleeping and throw it into the furnace of fire, in Jesus' Name, Amen!

Prayer Three

In the mighty name of Jesus Christ, I cover my mind, body, spirit and soul with the blood of Jesus Christ. I wear the helmet of salvation to cover my head and mind. My sight, hearing, smell and taste is covered under the protection of God. I decree and declare I have the mind of Christ. I am alert, knowledgeable, wise, confident and in tune with the instructions of God.

There is peace, clarity, love, joy and soundness in

my mind! I saturate my head, mind, thoughts and ideas with the blood of Jesus and protection of God. My mind will not be caged nor will it be unstable, tormented by fear, doubt or unbelief. Any voice that is not of God I command to be evicted out by the might power of Jesus Christ.

I rebuke every attack of the enemy to my head, mind and vision. I cancel every attack of headaches, negative thinking, mental programming and attachments, fear, doubt, worry, anxiety, poor concentration, forgetfulness, anxiety, poor choices and bad decisions. I destroy every cage designed to hinder my life, destiny and purpose.

I place my mind under the protection of Jesus Christ. I cancel every illusion the enemy wants me to see and evil voice he wants me to hear. I decree and declare that my eye see what God wants me to see, my ears hear the voice of God and what He wants me to hear alone. I have the mind of Christ and a sound mind, in Jesus name.

I restrict the enemy from attacking my head and mind in any way. I rebuke any force that attempts to bring sickness, injury, confusion and mental torment and command you to be destroyed by the fire of God immediately. The enemy plots of attacks against my mind I command to fail and not prosper. My mind will not be destroyed! My mind will not be caged! Jesus is the keeper of my mind.

I have the mind of Christ. My mind is healed, renewed, and restore, protected and it cannot be otherwise because Jesus is Lord. My thoughts are on things that are above, pure and good and my mind is stayed on God, therefore He keeps me in perfect peace. I walk in peace, I interact with peace and is shielded by the prince of peace. In Jesus Name! Amen.

Prayer Four

Dear Abba Father,

I embrace all my rights and authority as being your child today. Here and now Lord I am open to receive your spirit, guidance, wisdom, directions and instructions to walk as your son/daughter in your kingdom today. I decree and declare I am healed completely whole in you mentally, spiritually, emotionally and physically. I decree and declare I walk in the calling you have chosen for my life.

I decree and declare that my eyes, ears, nose, mouth, and mind function in alignment with your words. Today I take my rightful authority and rebuke every known and unknown plot of the enemy to hinder my growth, faith, and progress in you. Through Jesus I have been made new and whole and I walk in wholeness and completeness in you Heavenly Father, The Son Jesus Christ and the Holy Spirit. What I speak, decree and declare today, cannot be otherwise, In Jesus' Name.

Prayer Five

Father God,

I thank you for allowing Jesus Christ to be my lord and savior. Father this situation at hand is too heavy for me. I ask that you save me; save my mind, my body and soul. I lay this matter at your feet and ask for your help. You are my Lord, deliver me! Jesus, Fight for me! Fight for me oh, Lord! And Deliver me from my trouble.

Let there be light in my mind, light in my thoughts, light in my spirit and light in my soul, that I may see my way in the mist of darkness. Let your light illuminate me inside and out, as blanket of peace. In you and only in you do I find refuge. Deliver me, let there be light! Let there be light! In Jesus Mighty Name, Amen.

Prayer Six

Dear Jehovah Jireh

I thank you for being my everything. I love and adore you, seek to make you pleased with me. Thank you for being my Shepard, my provider, my way maker, deliver my shield and buckler. My life will not be caged. By your power I destroy every cage and move forward into the purpose you set before me. Thank you for changing my darkness into light.

Thank you for loving me when I did not even love myself. I never knew what love truly looked or felt like before you saved me. You are my first love and every day I seek to praise and worship in your presence. I command my mind, body, spirit and soul to bless you O, Lord and all that is within me. Thank you for covering mw with righteousness and renewing my strength.

As you transform my life, let my desire to pray forever be increased. May you destroy any force assigned to interfere with my prayer life. Give me the spirit and mind to pray without ceasing; a continuous fire that burns only for you, in Jesus' name, Amen!

Pray Strong!

Pray Long!

Pray Loud!

Pray in Silence!

Pray Sincerely!

Pray at All Times!

Pray with Expectation!

Pray in the Spirit!

Pray in Truth!

Pray In Confidence!

Pray thy kingdom come!

Pray God's Will Be Done!

Pray Persistently!

Pray Intentionally!

Pray Vigorously!

Pray with the Word!

Stay Encouraged!

Do It All In Faith! Be Blessed...

ABOUT UN-STUCKNES MINISTRIES

The purpose of Un-Stuckness Ministries is to help individuals who are emotionally and spiritually overwhelmed operate in their purpose, gifts and calling; and live an abundant life regardless of challenges.

Un-Stuckness Ministries is a faith-based business where God is at the center of it all. It was founded in 2016 by Minister Jamillah Cupe. She has a personal mission to **uproot** negative seeds that were planted by the enemy in the lives of individuals and families, and to **plant** seeds of life and hope: by the word of God, utilizing strategic techniques and prayers— that will rebuild and restore areas where one has been injured.

Jamillah accomplishes her mission through her books, speaking engagements, workshops and trainings. She teaches and demonstrates the redemption power of Jesus Christ to a population of those who find themselves stuck in life and are hungry for the knowledge and resources to surpass setbacks.

Jamillah passionately enjoys opportunities to inspire and teach individuals how to apply biblical principles as a way to address underlying everyday life challenges. She uses her educational credentials and ministry background to assist clients with achieving their personal goals. Her educational background is in Human Development and Family Studies, Criminal Justice, Criminology, Social Work and Child Development.

She is the author of *Un-Stuckness: Breaking Generational Chains and Stronghold Through Prayer* and *Un-Stuckness: Keys To Deliverance Through Prayer Jesus' Way* and more to come. You can gain more information about Un-Stuckness Ministries, its services and how to invite Jamillah to speak or facilitate a training, coaching or workshop sessions by visiting unstuckness.com.

Follow Jamillah on:
Facebook: @Jamillah Cupe Author Page
Instagram: @unstuckness_ministries_
Twitter: @jamillah_cupe
Email: unstuckness@gmail.com
Website: Unstuckness.com

Made in the USA
Middletown, DE
09 January 2020

82858638R00086